1. Introduction

Lending to small businesses in the United States fell dramatically after the onset of the Great Recession. Between the second quarter of 2008 and the second quarter of 2010, small business loans made by commercial banks declined by over $40 billion. Although part of this decline in new lending may be due to decreased demand of bank credit by firms, recent evidence suggests that much of it reflected changes in the supply of credit (Ivashina and Scharfstein 2010, Huang and Stephens 2011, Bassett et al. 2014). Similarly, the responses to the Federal Reserve's Senior Loan Officer Opinion Survey on Bank Lending Practices indicate that banks significantly tightened credit standards on Commercial and Industrial loans to firms between 2007 and 2009.[1]

The decline in small business lending has received much attention from policy makers and the media, especially because of its potential link to the high rate of unemployment. Indeed, more than 90% of all firms in the U.S. have fewer than ninety-nine employees, and they comprised roughly 35% of aggregate paid employment.[2] Unlike larger firms, which have broader access to capital markets, small businesses are highly dependent on bank financing.[3] An important implication is that any kind of disruption in the flow of bank credit may have significant real effects on the labor market.

In this paper we investigate the link between small business lending and unemployment during the Great Recession in the United States. We identify credit supply effects by using industry-level measures of external financial dependence following the work of Rajan and

---

[1] Small business lending figures are from Consolidated Reports of Condition and Income, where small business loans are defined as loans with original amounts of $1 million or less. The responses to the Senior Loan Officer Opinion Survey on Bank Lending Practices are from Figure 1 in the October 2011 report.

[2] See Hurst and Wild Pugsley (2011) for a detailed analysis using data from the Statistics of U.S. Businesses (SUSB) compiled by the U.S. Census Bureau for 2007.

[3] See, for example, Petersen and Rajan (1994), Cole, Wolken, and Woodburn (1996), Berger, Klapper, and Udell (2001).

Zingales (1998). If the reduction in small business lending affects employment, then workers in smaller firms are more likely to be affected, primarily those working in firms that depend on bank financing. We test our hypothesis by combining information on workers' firm size and employment status from the Current Population Survey with firms' financial information from Compustat and the Survey of Small Business Finance. We then estimate the likelihood of becoming unemployed during the recent financial crisis across industrial sectors with different degrees of external financial dependence, separately for small and large firms.

We find that during the Great Recession workers are more likely to become unemployed if they work in sectors with high external financial dependence. In these sectors the impact of the recession on the likelihood of becoming unemployed is stronger for workers in smaller firms. By contrast, we do not find significant differences in unemployment propensity between workers of small and large firms in sectors with low external financial dependence. These results are consistent with a credit supply shock that affected disproportionally more those workers in financially constrained firms during the recent financial crisis. A back of the envelope calculation suggests that these dynamics explain about 8% of the rise in the aggregate unemployment rate. The findings are robust to the exclusion of the construction sector and to using different measures of external financial dependence.

While these results are consistent with a credit supply shock hypothesis, an important potential confounding factor is a reduction on the demand side. Borrowers may be reluctant to expand their businesses, or may consider down-sizing because of changes in the demand for their goods and services during the recession. This would lead to a reduction in their demand for loans and an increase in layoffs of workers. This channel may explain our findings if the reduction in the demand falls primarily on small, bank-dependent firms. Our methodology is specifically designed to address this issue as we divide firms by external financial dependence at the industry level. If small firms suffer larger declines in demand for their goods there is no evident reason this should primarily happen in sectors with high external financial dependence.

To provide further support for our interpretation of the findings, we repeat our analyses around the 2001 recession and the Savings and Loan (S&L) crisis that led to the 1990-1991 recession. We exploit the fact that the 2001 recession did not originate in banks' balance sheets and was therefore not associated with a reduction in loan supply. The S&L crisis, on the other hand, did originate in the banking sector similarly to the Great Recession. If credit constraints are important in explaining transitions to unemployment during a downturn, we should find larger swings in unemployment for credit-constrained firms in 1990-91 but not in the 2001 recession.

The findings from the 2001 and 1990-1991 recessions are fully consistent with our hypothesis. The estimates around the 2001 recession show almost identical changes in unemployment among small and large firms in industries with high and low external financial dependence. However, the estimates for the 1990-1991 recession show very similar patterns to the estimates from the 2007-2010 analysis, where transition to unemployment is more pronounced among small firms in industries with high external financial dependence. For the 1990-1991 recessions we also exploit regional variation and focus on New England. The S&L crisis was especially virulent in New England, a region that experienced sharp declines in real estate prices and whose banks faced large capital declines due to their exposure to real estate (Peek and Rosengren 1994). The results from this exercise show a steeper increase in unemployment in New England as banks responded to their deteriorated financial condition by shrinking their balance sheets and reducing credit availability in a very similar fashion to the Great Recession.

All of these results are consistent with a credit supply contraction hypothesis and highlight the importance of banks' financial health for credit availability and their impact on the macroeconomy, along the lines of Bernanke (1983), Holmstrom and Tirole (1997), and Peek and Rosengren (2000). Our paper also reinforces the conclusions in Gertler and Gilchrist (1994), who find that growth in sales, inventories, and bank debt of small manufacturing firms is more sensitive to monetary policy shocks than that of larger firms. Similarly, these findings are consistent with a long list of studies that document the impact of credit constraints on investment spending, employment, and the fact that during recessions, industries with higher external financial dependence are hit harder in terms of production growth, value added, capital formation, and number of establishments.[4] Methodologically, our paper differs from these papers in that we differentiate firms by both size and external financial dependence. Another difference is that we examine changes in employment focusing on the recent financial crisis as well as the 2001 and 1990-91 recessions.

Our paper's key contribution is to emphasize the channels underlying the important role of finance in real economic activity, as we show that small businesses were laying off workers in the current recession due to credit constraints. This result naturally relates to the literature on the real effects of the credit supply shock during the Great Recession. Duchin et al (2010), for

---

[4] Examples include Fazzari, Hubbard, and Peterson 1988, Gertler and Hubbard 1988, Hoshi, Kashyap, and Scharfstein 1991, Whited 1992, Kashyap, Lamont, and Stein 1994, and Duchin, Ozbas, and Sensoy 2010; Sharpe 1994, Nickell and Nicolitsas 1999, Gozzi and Goetz 2010, Benmelech, Bergman, and Seru 2011, Bascim, Baskaya, and Kilinc 2011); Braun and Larrain 2005; Kroszner, Laeven, and Klingebiel 2007, and Dell'Ariccia, Detragiache, and Rajan 2008.

example, find that investment declines significantly more for firms with low cash reserves during the crisis. Similarly, Almeida et al (2012) find that firms vulnerable to refinancing at the peak of the financial crisis reduce investment spending and bypass attractive investment opportunities. A recent study of 1,050 Chief Financial Officers conducted by Campello, Graham, and Harvey (2010) also indicates that financially constrained firms planned deeper cuts in employment in the midst of the recent financial crisis. Chodorow-Reich (2014) is most complementary to our work as he finds that the withdrawal of credit played an important role in explaining the employment decline at small and medium firms in the year following the Lehman bankruptcy.

We also contribute to the literature that focuses on the role of small businesses in job creation and labor markets. The academic literature in this area has mixed findings. Haltiwanger, Jarmin, and Miranda (2010), for example, show that small firms do not create jobs faster once firm age is accounted for. On the other hand, Neumark, Wall, and Zhang (2011) find an inverse relationship between net growth rates and firm size, though not in the manufacturing sector. Similarly, Moscarini and Postel-Vinay (2009) find that small businesses create more jobs in periods of high unemployment and recessions. Our paper highlights the importance of credit availability to achieve this outcome.

In the next section we describe our empirical strategy, the data, and the construction of measures of external financial dependence by industrial sectors. In Section 3 we provide descriptive statistics of the data and present our main findings. Section 4 describes various robustness tests where we look at two additional recession episodes, construct an alternative measure of financing needs, and estimate changes in the number of establishments instead of changes in unemployment. We conclude the paper in Section 5.

2. Empirical Strategy and Data

2.1 Empirical Strategy

Our econometric analysis is based on a specification of the following form,

$$y_{ijst} = \alpha_{is}^d + x'_{ijst}\theta^d + \delta^d recession_t + \mu^d small_{ijst-1}$$
$$+ \rho^d (recession_t \times small_{ijst-1}) + \mu_{ijst}^d \qquad (1)$$

where y_{ijst} is an indicator that equals to one if person i – whose main industry of occupation in the previous year was j and who currently resides in state s – switched from employment to unemployment between the years $t-1$ and t.[5]

Employment in year $t-1$ means that the person was employed at some point during the previous year. Unemployment in year t means that the person is unemployed in the month of March of year t in the week before she was surveyed by the Current Population Survey. y_{ijst} takes the value of zero if person i is employed both in $t-1$ and t.[6]

α_{js} are industry-state fixed effects that control for industry-state time invariant observable and unobservable factors that impact the probability of switching from employment to unemployment. The vector of characteristics x controls for workers' observable differences in age, gender, ethnicity, and years of completed education.[7] Controlling for these characteristics is

---

[5] To capture potential churning between unemployment and out of the labor force for a given worker and the fact that a lot of adjustment might have been on this margin, we also look at the transition from employment to non-employment, defined to include both transitions into unemployment and out of labor force. The results of our analysis carry through as reported in Appendix Table A.1, panel A.

[6] Respondents to the Current Population Survey (CPS) self-report their employment status in the week before the interview. In the March supplement to the CPS, respondents are asked about the size of their main employer in the previous year. Respondents who provide information on the size of their main employer must have been employed at some point during the previous year, but there is no information on the exact period.

[7] In our specification ethnicity is an indicator that equals to one if the person is white and equals to zero otherwise. We use the following categories for years of completed education: 0-11, 12, 13-15, 16, and 17+. We use the categorical and not continuous version of years of completed education because of the redesign of the CPS in the early 1990s. See Polivka (1996) for details.

important because the propensity of becoming unemployed in the Great Recession has not been equal across age, gender, ethnicity, and education (See for example Elsby et al. 2010).

We analyze the transition from employment to unemployment around three recession episodes in the United States: July 1990 – March 1991, March – November 2001, and December 2007 – June 2009. For each recession, our analysis uses a two to three-year window around the recession. Importantly, we observe transition from employment to unemployment only in the month of March of every year. We estimate equation (1) separately for each recession episode. Thus, for the 1990 recession, the recession indicator in equation (1) equals to one in the years 1991-92 and equals to zero in the years 1988-90; for the 2001 recession, the indicators equals to one in the years 2001-02 and equals to zero in 1998-2000; finally, for the Great Recession we define the recession indicator as one for the years 2008-2010 and zero for the years 2005-2007.

We define small firms as firms with at most 99 employees and large firms with 100+ employees. Later in the analyses we have a more granular definition of firm size. Information about the size of the employer is reported by the Current Population Survey respondents and refers to the main employer in the year prior to the survey. The small-firm indicator in equation (1) accounts for the fact that during non-recession times the transition from employment to unemployment may differ by firm size. To capture the differences in transition to unemployment by firm size during a recession, we interact small-firm indicator with a recession indicator. This is the main variable of interest in our analyses.

The contribution of this paper is the analysis of transition from employment to unemployment for workers during an economic downturn by firm size and external financial dependence. We define external financial dependence as the proportion of capital expenditures financed with external funds and mark every industry as having either "high" or "low" dependence on external finance, as explained in the next section. The specification in equation (1), therefore, includes a full set of interaction terms between all the right-hand side variables and an indicator for being in an industry with high external financial dependence. For ease of illustration we represent the additional interaction terms in equation (1) by an upper index $d = \{low, high\}$ in all the regression parameters.

Thus, $\hat{\rho}^{low}$ estimates the impact of a recession on transition from employment to unemployment among workers in small firms relative to workers in large firms in industries with low external financial dependence, whereas $\hat{\rho}^{high}$ has the same interpretation for industries with high external financial dependence. Our main interest is in the difference between the two point estimates,

$$\hat{\rho}^{high} - \hat{\rho}^{low} \qquad (2)$$

The difference between the estimates exploits variation in unemployment propensity across three dimensions: time (before and after the recession), firm size (small and large), and external financial dependence (high and low). The third dimension is especially useful because it helps isolate factors that have a differential impact on unemployment by firm size. It is possible, for example, that the reduction in the demand for goods and services during the recession fell disproportionately more on small firms and therefore affected their workers' likelihood of becoming unemployed. The estimate in (2) differences out this potential effect as long as the reduction in the demand is not differential by firms' external financial dependence.

We estimate equation (1) using Ordinary Least Squares instead of Probit or Logit because of concerns of bias of nonlinear estimates with fixed effects.[8] When assessing the statistical

---

[8] We have state-industry fixed effects separately for small and large firms, resulting in more than 5,500 fixed effects. Nonlinear estimates using Probit or Logit with this number of fixed effects may lead to biased estimates. In a specification with significantly less fixed effects we obtained essentially identical results using Ordinary Least Squares, Probit, and Logit.

significance of the difference between $\hat{\rho}^{high}$ and $\hat{\rho}^{low}$, we cluster the standard errors by state and industry using the procedures in Liang and Zeger (1986) to adjust for potential group structure of the error term.[9]

2.2 Data

The unemployment status of workers is obtained from the Current Population Survey (CPS) conducted by the Bureau of the Census for the Bureau of Labor Statistics. Our primary source is the Annual Demographic Supplements to the CPS which are conducted every March because they include information about the size of each individual's main employer in the year prior to the survey and her industry of occupation. Firm size is important because it helps us to categorize workers into small and large firms in terms the number of employees in the firm. Similarly, industry information is necessary because it helps us to assign measures of external financial dependence at the industry level based on separate calculation using Compustat firms.[10]

The March CPS files include some demographics of respondents, like age, gender, ethnicity, years of completed education, and state of residence, allowing us to control for these characteristics in the regression analyses. We include in the CPS sample all adult civilians aged 16+ in the year prior the survey (the year of employment) who work for wages and salary in the

---

[9] See Moulton (1986) and Bertrand, Duflo, and Mullainathan (2004) for further discussion about biases of standard errors with grouped data.

[10] Ideally, we would like to analyze changes in hiring and layoffs instead of looking only at the transition from employment to unemployment. Unfortunately, except for the CPS, we were not able to find data that include both firm size and detailed industry information. The Business Employment Dynamics (BED) which contains information on job gains and losses for new/existing/closing establishments has information either by firm size or by industry, but not both. The Job Openings and Labor Turnover Survey (JOLTS) – which has information on job openings, hires, and separations – does not contain information on firm size. In the Business Dynamics Statistics (BDS) all the industries are collapsed into eight sectors. This aggregation is not granular enough to capture cross-industry heterogeneity in external financial dependence.

private sector. We only exclude respondents whose main industry of occupation is in the financial sector or agriculture. The CPS has a sampling weight that allows recovering the representativeness of the sample to the whole population.

Because the annual data do not capture short-term unemployment or employment spells and because even during the crisis the monthly flow rate from unemployment to employment was around 15-20 percent, we also use the monthly data around the March supplement and construct a semi-panel exploiting the panel dimension of the CPS: Individuals complete the survey during 4 consecutive months, then stop for 8 months, and finally are surveyed for 4 additional months the following year. As noted above, only the March supplement asks for the size of the firm. Therefore, to construct the monthly panel, we are bound to use individuals that are interviewed in March. For these individuals, we have information on their employment status up to 3 months before or after March. Therefore, we can construct a monthly semi-panel around the March data. The main advantage of using the monthly panel is that it allows capturing individuals who switch from unemployment to employment (or vice versa) around March. For example, an individual who was employed in March, then switched jobs and stayed unemployed while looking for a job, and then she was employed during the next March survey. The annual data would not capture this transition, while the monthly panel does.

Despite the use of a monthly panel, the analysis is subject to limitations. Each worker's firm size is available in the year prior to the survey only if she was employed at least for some time in that year. Thus, firm size information is not available for individuals who were unemployed for the entire year prior to the survey. This implies that long term unemployment spells are not captured in our calculations, which may underestimate the role of financing constraints. Moreover, because we are estimating transition to unemployment, we are concerned about not capturing individuals who were unemployed during the entire previous year but are currently employed. The fraction of such individuals is not large, however, and does not affect our main results. We show this by assuming two extreme cases: first, we assigned all such workers to small firms, and second, to large firms. Making these two assumptions does not change our main findings.

Given these data limitations in the CPS, we supplement our main analysis by looking at the impact of the Great Recession on the number of establishments, differentially by firm size and external financial dependence. We use data from the County Business Patterns (CBP), which is an annual count of establishments at the county level. Importantly, the CBP counts establishments by firm size and industry (3-digit NAICS). We sum the total number of establishments in a given state, year, and industry separately for small and large firms and divide the total number of establishments by the state population. We use the natural logarithm of the number of establishments per capita as the left-hand side variable in a specification similar to equation (1). As in the CPS, we define small firms as firms with at most 99 employees and assign measures of external financial dependence to the industrial sectors in the CBP using figures from Compustat.[11]

Information on the external financial dependence of the different industrial sectors is based on data from Compustat. To construct this measure, which was originally proposed by Rajan and Zingales (1998), we follow the procedures described in Cetorelli and Strahan (2006) and define external financial dependence as the proportion of capital expenditures financed with external funds.[12] A positive value indicates that firms must issue debt or equity to finance investments,

---

[11] The mapping between the industrial sectors in these two data is provided in Table O.1 in the online appendix available on the author's webpage.

[12] We use firms that have been on Compustat for at least 10 years between the years 1980 and 1996. The reason for this choice is to capture firms' demand for credit and not the amount of credit supplied to them. It has been widely

whereas a negative value indicates that firms have free cash and, therefore, no external financing needs. We match the two-digit SIC categories in Compustat to the industrial categories in the CPS.[13] Following Rajan and Zingales (1998), we argue there is a technological reason why some industries depend more on external finance than others. For example, industries may differ in the scale of the initial project, the gestation period, the cash harvest period, and the requirement for continuing investment. These technological factors determine the demand for external financing. It implies that, ceteris paribus, industries such as pipelines, metal mining, and home furniture – which require a lot of external funding – should be more affected by a credit supply shock than industries like leather and leather products, insurance carriers, and forestry.[14]

As a robustness check, we also calculate industries' bank dependence using the 1998 Survey of Small Business Finance (SSBF). After all, our EFD measure, which is calculated using publicly traded and thus relatively large firms, may not capture the bank dependence of small firms as well. In fact, the correlation between this measure of bank dependence and our external financial dependence measure, while positive, is only about 10 percent. So, using this additional survey, for each firm, we construct this additional bank dependence measure by calculating the share of assets financed with debt from financial institutions for each firm.[15] Bank dependence in each two-digit SIC category is equal to the median value of firms' share of assets financed with debt. Bank dependence is constructed for all industrial sectors in the SSBF and then matched to the industrial categories in the CPS.

---

documented that young firms are financially constrained and their debt is likely to be determined by the amount of credit offered to them and not by the optimal equity-to-debt ratio (see e.g., Fazzari et al 1988).

[13] See Table O.2 in the online appendix available on the author's webpage.

[14] Appendix Table A.2 reports measures of external financial dependence for each of the 60 industrial sectors in our sample.

[15] Debt includes loans, capital leases and lines of credit, as well as personal mortgages. We use the limits on the lines of credit to better capture the supply of credit to those businesses.

3. Results

3.1 Descriptive Statistics

Table 1 reports mean characteristics of Compustat firms by the median external financial dependence (EFD) of their industry. The table shows that growth of assets, capital expenditures, and sales for firms in low EFD industries is somewhat larger than firms with high EFD during the period 1980-1996. For example, the average real growth rate of assets of low EFD firms over the period 1980-1996 is 4.5% versus 1.9% for high EFD firms. However, the difference in growth rates of assets between the two groups of firms is statistically insignificant (column 3). The differences in growth rates of capital expenditures and sales between high and low EFD industries are insignificant as well. These figures suggest that the greater demand for external finance does not seem to reflect greater growth or investment opportunities. Instead, external finance reflects differences in financing needs mainly due to industry level technological reasons as was initially argued by Rajan and Zingales (1998).

Table 2 reports mean characteristics of workers by firm size and external financial dependence. We compare workers' age, gender, ethnicity, and years of completed education across small and large firms, separately for industries with high and low external financial dependence based on their responses to the 2005 March Current Population Survey. We find that small firms in both low and high EFD industries have slightly older workers and a higher percentage of workers who identify themselves as white. In industries with high external financial dependence, small firms have slightly more high-school drop-outs (4 percentage point difference). The gender composition across small and large firms is statistically identical.

The important result emerging from Table 2 is that differences in workers' characteristics between small and large firms are similar in industries with low and high external financial dependence. The "balancing" of workers' characteristics across firm size and external financial dependence is important for our analyses because it helps to rule out the possibility that workers in small firms in industries with high external financial dependence are more likely to become unemployed because they have different characteristics. For example, the wage comparison between workers in small and large firms shows that workers in larger firms earn more than workers in smaller firms, with an average gap of about $2.00 per hour. This may lead to the possibility that workers in large firms are more skilled and are able to find jobs faster. The key for our identification strategy, however, is the difference in the wage gap across industries with high and low external financial dependence. Table 2 shows that in industries with low external financial dependence the wage gap is $2.22 and in industries with high external financial dependence the gap is $2.29. The difference in the wage gaps is insignificant (column 7). This provides comfort that the main results in the paper are not driven by selection.

3.2 Main Results

Our empirical strategy is to emphasize the differential impact of the Great Recession on the probability of transition to unemployment using the variation in firm size and financing needs. We illustrate this strategy in Table 3 using the specification in equation (1).

All estimates in Panel A of Table 3 are from a single regression. For ease of illustration we present the results as follows: the columns of the table are divided by workers' firm size and external financial dependence (EFD) of their industry; the rows show the differences between the columns. Small firms are firms with 1-99 employees, whereas large firms have at least 100 employees. Industries with low external financial dependence are industries with below median EFD.

The first two columns indicate an almost identical increase of 2.5 percentage points in unemployment propensity among workers in small and large firms in industries with low EFD. The next two columns, on the other hand, show that the recession has a more pronounced impact on the probability of becoming unemployed for workers in high EFD industries. In these industries, the unemployment likelihood among workers of small firms increased by 3.8 percentage points compared to 2.5 in large firms. This is a difference of 1.3 percentage points. The second row of the table shows that this difference is statistically significant at a 1% confidence level.

The third row of Table 3 exploits variation across the dimensions of firm size and external financial dependence by taking the difference between the two differences in the second row. In the notation of equation (2) this difference is,

$$\hat{\rho}^{high} - \hat{\rho}^{low} = (.038 - .025) - (.025 - .025) = .013$$

The point estimate of .013 means that the relative (small vs large) impact of the recession on unemployment propensity is 1.3 percentage points larger in industries with high financing needs. This difference is statistically significant and economically large.[16]

Panel B of Table 3 reports the results using the monthly CPS data. The number of observations increases substantially because now we have monthly information for the same individuals that were in the annual data. Both data sets include the March observation for each individual. The monthly panel also includes the months before or after March for those individuals surveyed in March. While it is hard to compare the magnitude of the coefficients from the annual and the monthly analysis, it is important to note that the estimates are

---

[16] We also find a similar pattern with respect to the transition out of the labor force, i.e. when we include not just the transition from employment to unemployment but also the transition from employment to non-participation as reported in panel (A) of Appendix Table A.1.

qualitatively similar.[17] The coefficient for the small firms in high EFD industries (.035) is the largest coefficient and is statistically different from the other coefficients, consistent with the results based on the annual data.

Our interpretation of the findings is that financing constraints played an important role in explaining changes in unemployment during the Great Recession. An alternative interpretation, however, is that the recession was especially harmful for the demand for goods and services produced by small businesses. And perhaps the drop in demand was especially steep for small businesses in industries with high external financial dependence.

We explore this possibility across two dimensions. First, we account for industry-state fixed effects, thus estimating the changes in unemployment in small versus large firms within the same industry and state. The identifying assumption here is that changes in demand are not differential by firm size within an industry in any given state.

Second, we exclude the construction sector from the analysis realizing that the construction sector has especially suffered during the recession. Panel (B) in Appendix Table A.1 shows the results from this exercise. The construction sector has external financial dependence above the median and thus the results in the first two columns Table A.1 are identical to the results in Panel A of Table 3. In high EFD industries, changes in unemployment are smaller for workers in both small and large firms once the construction workers are excluded. Nevertheless, the differential impact of the recession by firm size is significant (.028 − .020 = .008) both statistically and economically. The difference between high and low external financial dependence (.008 − (.000)

---

[17] Recall that our annual analysis is not able to capture individuals who may transition in and out of employment within the past year. Similarly, in our monthly analysis, while we can capture such short-term dynamics, we are only able to do so within a given 4-month window. Moreover, even if the monthly analysis is likely to capture a higher number of unemployment spells which would be missing from the annual analysis, it is not at all clear why the coefficient of interest (the differential effect by firm size and EFD) should be larger or smaller in the monthly analysis.

= .008) is significant as well, indicating that our core findings hold when we exclude the construction sector.

Despite these findings, our main result may still be confounded by some demand effects. Our EFD measure intends to capture the technology used at the industry level. However, small firms within a given industry may use a technology that is actually very different from the one used by their larger counterparts in the same industry. Similarly, small business may be concentrated in industries with smaller natural scales (Hurst and Wild Pugsley 2011). Therefore, it is plausible that small and large firms within a given industry and state may have received different demand shocks during the recession and, in that case, they would be affected differently by the credit crunch. In order to reinforce our interpretation of the results, we conduct additional robustness checks in the following sections.

3.3 Monotonicity Analysis

So far we have split workers into two buckets of firm size (small and large) and two buckets of external financial dependence (high and low). In this section we break both firm size and external financial dependence into three categories. If changes in unemployment are driven by changes in the supply of credit, we expect the probability of unemployment to increase monotonically with external financial dependence and to decline monotonically with respect to firm size.

To test the monotonicity of our findings with respect to firm size and external financial dependence (EFD), we plot the changes in workers' unemployment propensity in 2008-2010 relative to 2005-2007 in Figure 1. First, in panel (a) and (b), instead of separating firms into only two categories, we split the sample into three equal-sized buckets based on the distribution of external financial dependence. Workers in the lowest 33 percentiles of the EFD distribution belong to the "low" EFD bucket, whereas workers in the top 33 percentiles fall into the "high" EFD bucket. Workers between the 34th and the 66th percentiles are in the "medium" category. As before, we separate firms by two categories of firm size: 1-99 versus 100+ employees. The bars in Figure 1 represent point estimates of δ from the following specification:

$$y_{ijst} = \alpha_{js} + x'_{ijst}\theta + \delta recession_t + \mu_{ijst} \qquad (3)$$

where, as before, y_{ijst} is an indicator that equals to one if person i – whose main industry of occupation in the previous year was j and who currently resides in state s – switched from employment to unemployment between the years $t - 1$ and t. α_{js} are industry-state fixed effects and the vector of characteristics x controls for workers' observable differences in age, gender, ethnicity, and years of completed education. Finally, *recession* takes the value of unity in the years 2008-2010 and equals zero in the years 2005-2007. We estimate equation (3) using Ordinary Least Squares. We use sampling weights provided by the CPS to ensure representativeness of our sample.

We estimate δ in equation (3) six times for each category of firm size and for the three groups of external financial dependence. The results, shown in panels (a) and (b) of Figure 1, show that during the recession the unemployment propensity is changing *monotonically* with the degree of external financial dependence but *only* for small firms. In particular, we find that workers of small firms in low EFD industries were 2.1 percentage points more likely to become unemployed compared to 2.6 percentage points in the medium EFD and 3.6 percentage points in the high EFD group. However, for large firms, there is no evidence for a monotonic relationship between the likelihood of becoming unemployed and external financial dependence.

Next, we test the monotonicity of our findings with respect to firm size. Specifically, we separate firms into three categories of size based on the number of employees: 1-99, 100-499, and 500+, and separate industries by the median external financial dependence. So, this time we estimate equation (3) separately for each of the two categories of external financial dependence and three categories of firm size.

The results are presented in panels (c) and (d) of Figure 1. The figures show a clear-cut monotonic relationship between the propensity of becoming unemployed and firm size in high EFD industries. The largest changes in unemployment are for workers of the smallest firms (1-99 employees), whereas the smallest changes are for those in the largest firms (500+ employees). In particular, a high EFD industry worker in a firm with 1-99 employees is 3.2 percentage points more likely to become unemployed during the crisis, compared to 2.9 percentage points for those working in firms with 100-499 employees, and 1.9 percentage points in firms with 500+ employees. In industries with low external financial dependence, on the other hand, there is no relationship between firm size and the likelihood of becoming unemployed during the recession.

These monotonicity analyses provide further evidence for the channels that drove the transitions to unemployment during the 2008-2010 financial crisis. In particular, we find a monotonic relationship between firm size and changes in unemployment propensity. Importantly, this relationship holds only for industries with high external financial dependence. Similalrly, we find a monotonic relationship between external financial dependence and changes in unemployment. Strikingly, this relationship holds only for smaller firms.

3.4 Contribution to Aggregate Unemployment

To get a sense of how much of the increase in the overall unemployment rate, which doubled from 5.0 percent in December 2007 to 10.0 percent in December 2009 (BLS), can be attributed to financial constraints of small firms, we first estimate how many workers were in small firms in high EFD industries. According to BLS, total employment in the U.S. in December 2007 was

146,273,000 people. Applying the share of workers in small firms in high EFD industries computed from CPS data (31%), we obtain that 45,344,630 people were working in these firms.

Multiplying this number by the differential transition probability from employment to unemployment reported in Table 3 (1.3%), we estimate that an additional 589,480 people became unemployed due to financial constraints at small firms. According to BLS, the number of unemployed in the U.S. was 7,645,000 people in December 2007 and the total U.S. labor force was 153,120,000 people in December 2009. Hence, our estimates suggest that an increase of 589,480 would cause the number of unemployed to go up to 8,234,480 and the unemployment rate to increase from 5.0% in December 2007 to 5.4% in December 2009 due to financial constraints of small firms in high EFD industries. Relative to an overall rise of 5 percentage points, this implies that the credit supply shock explains about 8% of the overall increase in unemployment rate during the recession.

4. Robustness Tests

4.1 Other Recessions

So far our findings indicate that the financial crisis of 2007-2010 is especially harmful for small firms in industries with high financing needs. Our interpretation is that changes in unemployment in these firms are driven by changes in the supply of credit. To provide further evidence for this hypothesis we repeat our empirical exercise for the 2001 recession and for the Savings and Loan (S&L) crisis that led to the 1990-1991 recession.

The 2001 recession was triggered by the bursting of the bubble in the technological sector and did not originate in banks' balance sheets. The 2001 recession, therefore, serves as a "placebo" test: if changes in unemployment in small, financially constrained firms are driven by changes in the supply of credit, then we should find no differential impact of the 2001 recession on unemployment by firm size and external financial dependence.

The S&L crisis, on the other hand, originated in the banking sector and was related to problems in the real estate. The resulting credit crunch and the recession in 1990-1991 provide an ideal scenario to test the robustness of our findings. If credit supply contraction is important in driving the transition to unemployment for bank-dependent firms, then our estimates around the 1990-1991 recession should be similar to the estimates around the recent financial crisis.

In addition, the 1990-91 recession was characterized by a strong geographical component, with New England being the most affected region (Peek and Rosengren 1994). We exploit this regional variation by estimating the transition to unemployment separately for New England. We expect small, financially constrained firms in New England to be especially affected by the 1990-1991 recession.

We start with the 2001 recession in Panel A of Table 4. The specification here is identical to Table 3, except that the *recession* indicator now takes the value of unity in the years 2001-2002 and takes the value of zero in the years 1998-2000. We find that in industries with low external financial dependence, workers are 0.6 percentage points more likely to become unemployed if they work for small firms and 1.2 percentage points if they work for large firms. The difference between the two estimates is statistically significant. In industries with high external financial dependence, the probability of unemployment increased by 0.6 and 0.8 percentage points for small and large firms, respectively. This difference is statistically insignificant. More importantly, the difference of the differences ($-.003 - (-.007) = .004$) is insignificant as well, indicating that financing constraints become insignificant in explaining the unemployment patterns of small or large firms during the 2001 recession.

In Panel B of Table 4 we analyze the results for the 1990-1991 recession. The *recession* indicator in this table takes the value of unity in the years 1991-1992 and takes the value of zero in the years 1988-1990. Similarly to the analysis of the Great Recession, workers in small firms in industries with high financing needs are primarily affected by the 1990-91 recession. The difference between small and large firms in high EFD industries (1.3 percentage points) is statistically different from the same difference in low EFD industries (−0.4 percentage points) and is also economically large.

In Table 5 we turn to the regional analysis of the 1990-1991 recession. The specifications in this table are identical to Panel B of Table 4, except for the separation of the results by regions. In panel A we report the results only for New England and in panel B for the other regions. Consistent with the fact that the credit crunch was more severe in New England, workers in small firms in industries with high financing needs in New England have the steepest rise in unemployment during the 1990-1991 recession. This increase was larger than for workers in corresponding firms in regions outside of New England and in industries with low external financial dependence within New England. These results further reinforce the credit supply channel.

We graphically illustrate our findings through the various recessions in Figure 2. We plot the year-by-year proportion of workers who switched from employment to unemployment between the years t and $t - 1$ by firm size and external financial dependence using the March Current Population Surveys from 1988 to 2011. The left plot is for industries with low EFD and the right plot is for high EFD industries. The solid lines represent workers in small firms (1-99 employees), while the dashed lines are for workers in large firms (100+ employees).

This figure depicts the results we are capturing in the regressions. Clearly, the transition to unemployment increases during recessions. However, there are remarkable differences across firm size and external financial dependence. For industries with low financing needs, the unemployment trends for workers in small and large firms move very closely. In industries with high financing needs, on the other hand, the transition to unemployment during recessions increases much more for smaller firms.

4.2 Bank Dependence

So far our analyses have relied on measures of external financial dependence based on mature Compustat firms. As a robustness check we construct an alternative measure of financing needs using the 1998 Survey of Small Business Finance (SSBF). The SSBF measure of financial dependence captures bank dependence more accurately than the measure based on Compustat because it is based on small firms which primarily use bank loans. However, the SSBF-based measure of bank dependence mixes demand for credit and supply of credit because it is based on a survey of *small* firms. Nevertheless, we find it helpful to use an additional measure of dependence on bank financing as a robustness check. We split the industries by the median dependence on banks. Industries with below median bank dependence have low bank dependence, whereas industries with above median bank dependence have high bank dependence.

The results in Table 6 are very similar to the results in Table 3 where we used theCompustat-based measure of financing needs. As before, we find no differential impact of the Great Recession on unemployment by firm size in industries with low bank dependence. Using the annual data (Panel A), we find that the difference is equal to .004 percentage points (.024 − .019) which is not statistically different from zero. In industries with high bank dependence, on the other hand, the probability of becoming unemployed rises by 1.5 percentage points (.047 − .033) more for workers in small firms. The difference of the differences (.015 − .004) is statistically significant at the 5% level and is very similar in magnitude to the corresponding difference in Table 3. We obtain very similar results when using the monthly CPS panel data (Panel B). Overall, the results in Table 6 show that our core findings are robust to the measure of financial dependence.

4.3 Number of Establishments

One of the limitations of our analyses in this paper is that we focus only on the transition of workers from employment to unemployment, thus missing other important margins. The reason for this limitation is data availability as we describe in detail in the Data Section. Looking only at one margin becomes especially binding when thinking about policies to help the labor market where unemployment rate remains at a very high level.

In order to obtain a more complete picture, we complement our core findings by analyzing changes in the number of establishments from the County Business Patterns. The idea is to use the change in the number of establishments as a measure that combines changes in both employment and unemployment. We estimate a model similar to our baseline specification in equation (1) with the exception that the dependent variable is the natural logarithm of the number of establishments per capita in a given industry, state, and year. Another exception is that we do not control for the vector of workers' characteristics, x, as we are analyzing differences across establishments and not workers.

Table 7 shows the number of establishments that contracted during the Great Recession. We also find that this contraction was steeper among firms in industries with high external financial dependence, especially for smaller firms. Specifically, in these industries, the number of establishments among large firms dropped by 4.0 percent compared to 5.2 percent among small firms. In contrast, the contraction was significantly smaller in industries with low financing needs and very similar between large and small firms (3.6 and 3.5 percent, respectively). The difference of the small–large differences ($-.012 - .001$) is statistically significant at the 5% level. This finding highlights the importance of financial constraints from an aggregate perspective.

5. Conclusion

This paper shows that financing constraints of small firms are important drivers of unemployment dynamics around the Great Recession. In particular, workers in small firms in industries with high external financial dependence were more likely to become unemployed during the financial crisis than workers in large firms in the same industries. On the other hand, we do not find significant differences in unemployment between workers in small and large firms in sectors with low external financial dependence. These results suggest that the reduction in bank lending during the Great Recession disproportionally affected small firms that are highly dependent on external financing.

To provide additional assurance that we are capturing credit supply shocks and not changes in demand, we also examine the 1990-91 and the 2001 recessions in the U.S. For the 1990-91 recession, we find very similar results to the Great Recession, namely larger changes in unemployment among workers in small firms in industries with high external financial dependence. Moreover, we find especially significant impact on workers in New England where banks were disproportionally affected by the Savings and Loan crisis. The 2001 recession, on the other hand, had no differential impact on unemployment by firm size and external financial dependence. This is in line with our expectations because the 2001 recession was concentrated in the technological sector, and unlike the 1990-91 recession banks were largely unaffected.

This paper indicates that financing constraints of small firms were one of the important drivers of unemployment dynamics in the U.S. during the Great Recession. The resulting policy implications are especially important. We suggest that policies aimed at making credit available to small firms, such as loans guaranteed by the Small Business Administration, would help stabilize the labor markets and economic activity in the United States.

References

Almeida, H., M. Campello, B. Laranjeira, and S. Weisbenner. 2012. Corporate Debt Maturity and the Real Effects of the 2007 Credit Crisis. Critical Finance Review 1, 3-58.

Basci E., Y. S. Baskaya, and M. Kilinc. 2011. Financial Shocks and Industrial Employment. Central Bank of the Republic of Turkey Working Papers 1112.

Bassett, W. F., M. B. Chosak, J. C. Driscoll, and E. Zakrajsek. 2014. Changes in Bank Lending Standards and the Macroeconomy. Journal of Monetary Economics 62, 23-40.

Benmelech, E., N. K. Bergman, and A. Seru. 2011. Financing Labor. National Bureau of Economic Research Working Paper 17144.

Berger, A. N., L. F. Klapper, and G. F. Udell. 2001. The Ability of Banks to Lend to Informationally Opaque Small Businesses. Journal of Banking and Finance 25(12), 2127-67.

Bernanke, Ben S. 1983. Nonmonetary Effects of the Financial Crisis in the Propagation of the Great Depression. American Economic Review 73(3), 257-76.

Bertrand, M., E. Duflo, and S. Mullainathan. 2004. How Much Should We Trust Differences-in-Differences Estimates? Quarterly Journal of Economics 119(1), 249-75.

Braun, M., and B. Larrain. 2005. Finance and the Business Cycle: International, Inter-Industry Evidence. Journal of Finance 60(3), 1097-1128.

Campello, M., J. R. Graham, and C. R. Harvey. 2010. The Real Effects of Financial Constraints: Evidence from a Financial Crisis. Journal of Financial Economics 97(3), 470-87.

Cetorelli, N., and P. E. Strahan. 2006. Finance as a Barrier to Entry: Bank Competition and Industry Structure in Local U.S. Markets. Journal of Finance 61(1), 437-61.

Chodorow-Reich, G. 2014. The Employment Effects of Credit Market Disruptions: Firm-level Evidence from the 2008-09 Financial Crisis. Quarterly Journal of Economics 129(1), 1-59.

Cole, R. A., J. D. Wolken, and R. L. Woodburn. 1996. Bank and Nonbank Competition for Small Business Credit: Evidence from the 1987 and 1993 National Surveys of Small Business Finances. Federal Reserve Bulletin 82, 983-95.

Dell'Ariccia, G., E. Detragiache, and R. Rajan. 2008. The Real Effect of Banking Crises. Journal of Financial Intermediation 17(1), 89-112.

Duchin, R., O. Ozbas, and B. A. Sensoy. 2010. Costly External Finance, Corporate Investment, and the Subprime Mortgage Credit Crisis. Journal of Financial Economics 97(3), 418-35.

Elsby, M., B. Hobijn, and A. Sahin. 2010. The Labor Market in the Great Recession. Brookings Papers on Economic Activity, 1-48.

Fazzari, S. M., R. G. Hubbard, and B. C. Peterson. 1988. Financing Constraints and Corporate Investment. Brookings Papers on Economic Activity, 141-206.

Gertler, M., and S. Gilchrist. 1994. Monetary Policy, Business Cycles, and the Behavior of Small Manufacturing Firms. Quarterly Journal of Economics 109(2), 309-40.

Gertler, M., and R. G. Hubbard. 1988. Financial Factors in Business Fluctuations. National Bureau of Economic Research Working Paper 2758.

Gozzi, J. C., and M, Goetz. 2010. Liquidity Shocks, Local Banks, and Economic Activity: Evidence from the 2007-2009 Crisis. Unpublished.

Haltiwanger, J., R. Jarmin, and J. Miranda. 2010. Who Creates Jobs? Small vs. Large vs. Young. National Bureau of Economic Research Working Paper 16300.

Holmstrom, B. and J. Tirole. 1997. Financial Intermediation, Loanable Funds, and the Real Sector. Quarterly Journal of Economics 112(3), 663-91.

Hoshi, T., A. Kashyap, and D. Scharfstein. 1991. Corporate Structure, Liquidity, and Investment: Evidence from Japanese Industrial Groups. Quarterly Journal of Economics 106(1), 33-60.

Huang, H,, and E. Stephens. 2011. From Housing Bust to Credit Crunch: Evidence from Small Business Loans. Unpublished.

Hurst, E., and B. Pugsley. 2011. What Do Small Businesses Do?" Brookings Papers on Economic Activity, 73-118.

Ivashina, V. and D. Scharfstein. 2010. Bank Lending During the Financial Crisis of 2008. Journal of Financial Economics 97(3), 319-38.

Kashyap, A. K., O. A. Lamont, and J. C. Stein. 1994. Credit Conditions and the Cyclical Behavior of Inventories. Quarterly Journal of Economics 109(3), 565-92.

Kroszner, Randall S., L. Laeven, and D. Klingebiel. 2007. Banking Crises, Financial Dependence, and Growth. Journal of Financial Economics 84(1), 187-228.

Liang, K., and S. L. Zeger. 1986. Longitudinal Data Analysis Using Generalized Linear Models. Biometrika 73(1), 13-22.

Moscarini, G., and F. Postel-Vinay. 2009. Large Employers are More Cyclically Sensitive. National Bureau of Economic Research Working Paper 14740.

Moulton, B. R. 1986. Random Group Effects and the Precision of Regression Estimates. Journal of Econometrics 32(3), 385-97.

Neumark, D., B. Wall, and J. Zhang. 2011. Do Small Businesses Create More Jobs? New Evidence for the United States from the National Establishment Time Series. Review of Economics and Statistics 93(1), 16-29.

Nickell, S., and D. Nicolitsas. 1999. How Does Financial Pressure Affect Firms? European Economic Review 43(8), 1435-56.

Peek, J., and E. S. Rosengren. 1994. Bank Real Estate Lending and the New England Credit Crunch. Real Estate Economics 22(1), 33-58.

Peek, J., and E. S. Rosengren. 2000. Collateral Damage: Effects of the Japanese Bank Crisis on Real Activity in the United States. American Economic Review 90(1), 30-45.

Petersen, M.A., and R. G. Rajan. 1994. The Benefits of Lending Relationships: Evidence from Small Business Data. Journal of Finance 49(1), 3-37.

Polivka, A. E. 1996. Data Watch: The Redesigned Current Population Survey. Journal of Economic Perspectives 10(3), 169-180.

Rajan, R. G., and L. Zingales. 1998. Financial Dependence and Growth. American Economic Review 88(3), 559-86.

Sharpe, S. A. 1994. Financial Market Imperfections, Firm Leverage, and the Cyclicality of Employment. American Economic Review 84(4), 1060-74.

Whited, T. M. 1992. Debt, Liquidity Constraints, and Corporate Investment: Evidence from Panel Data. Journal of Finance 47(4), 1425-60.

Figure 1 – Monotonicity by External Financial Dependence and Firm Size

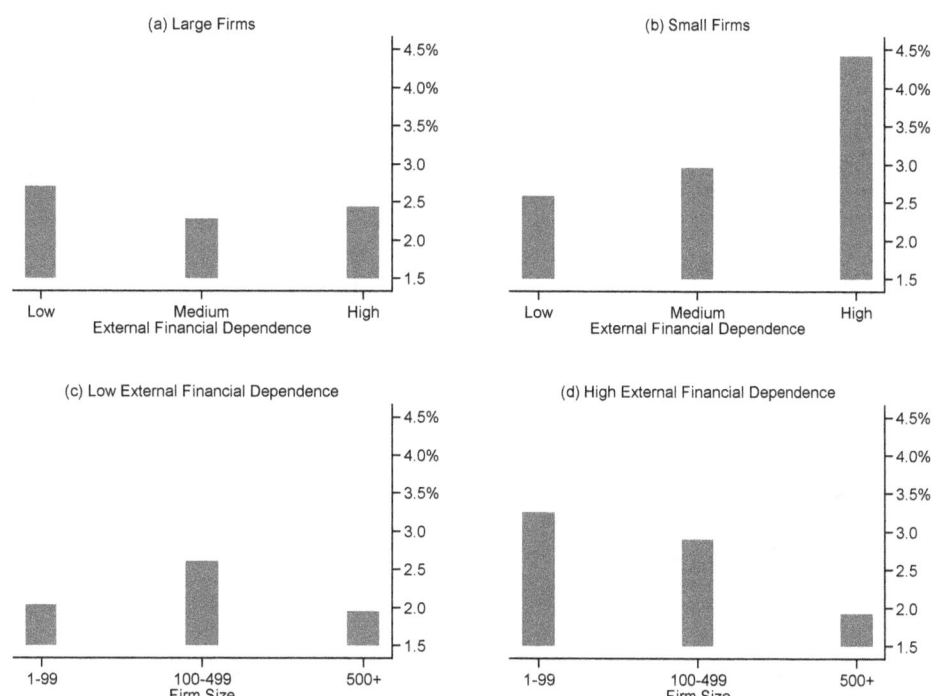

Note - The plots show changes in unemployment rate following the 2007 recession by external financial dependence and firm size. The upper plots are divided into three categories based on the distribution external financial dependence: below the 33rd percentile, 34th-66th percentile, and 67th percentile and above. Plot (a) includes firms with at least 100 employees, whereas plot (b) includes firms with at most 99 employees. The lower plots are divided into three categories of firm size based on the number of workers in the firm: 1-99, 100-499, and 500+. Plot (c) includes industries with below median external financial dependence. Plot (d) includes industries with external financial dependence above the median. External financial dependence equals the proportion of capital expenditures financed with external funds. External financial dependence is calculated using mature Compustat firms for the period 1980-1996. The bars represent estimates from 12 separate OLS regression where the dependent variables is an indicator that equals to one if a person transitioned from employment to unemployment between years $t-1$ and t. Each regression controls for workers' characteristics and state-industry (2-digit SIC) fixed effects. Workers' characteristics include age, gender, ethnicity, and years of completed education (0-11 years, 12, 13-15, or 16). All estimates are weighted by sampling weights provided by the Current Population Survey.

Figure 2 – Likelihood of Transition from Employment to Unemployment

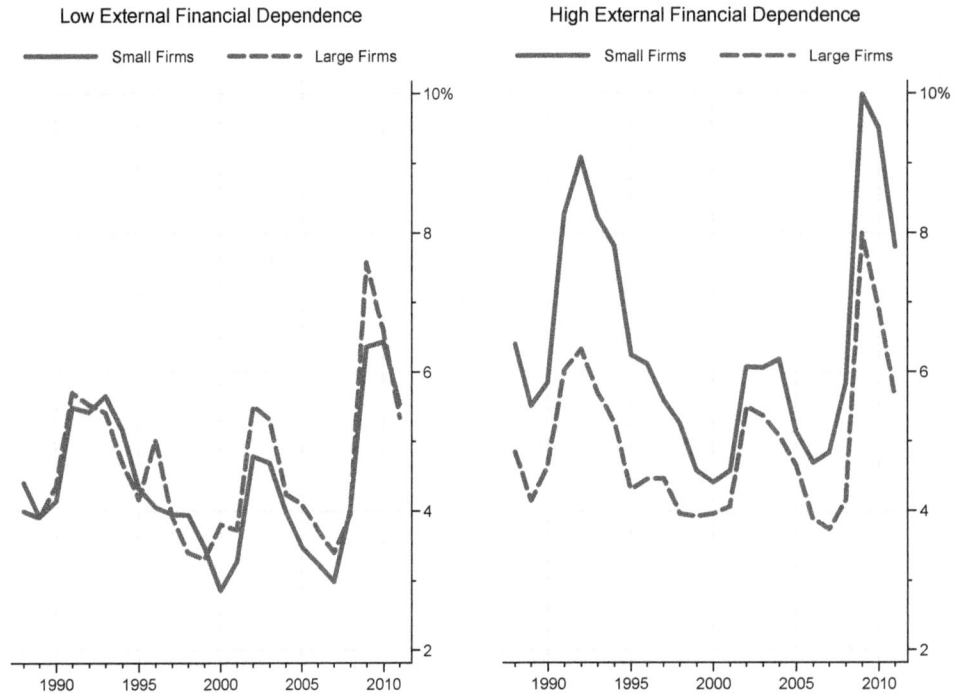

Note - The plots show year-by-year proportion of workers who switched from employment to unemployment between years *t* and *t-1* by firm size and external financial dependence. "Small" firms have at most 99 employees. External financial dependence equals the proportion of capital expenditures financed with external funds. A negative value (low external financial dependence) indicates that firms have free cash flow. A positive value indicates that firms must issue debt or equity to finance their investment. External financial dependence is calculated at 2-digit Standard Industrial Classification codes using mature Compustat firms for the period 1980-1996 using the procedures described in Cetorelli and Strahan [2006].

Source - March Current Population Surveys, 1988-2011.

Table 1 – Mean Characteristics of Firms by External Financial Dependence

	External Financial Dependence		
	Low (1)	High (2)	Difference (3)
Assets growth	.045	.019	-.026
			(.016)
Capital expenditures growth	.201	.134	-.067
			(.082)
Sales growth	.066	.042	-.024
			(.031)

Note - The table reports characteristics of Compustat firms by external financial dependence of their industry. Column (3) reports the difference between the first two columns. Robust standard errors are in parentheses. The results are based on 4,847 mature Compustat firms in the years 1980-1996. Mature firms are firms that have been in Compustat for at least 10 years. The growth rates of assets, capital expenditures, and sales are median values of year-to-year real ($1997, CPI adjusted) growth rates over the period 1980-1996. External financial dependence equals the proportion of capital expenditures financed with external funds. A negative value (low external financial dependence) indicates that firms have free cash flow. A positive value indicates that firms must issue debt or equity to finance their investment. External financial dependence is calculated at a 2-digit Standard Industrial Classification codes using mature Compustat firms for the period 1980-1996 using the procedures described in Cetorelli and Strahan (2006).

Table 2 – Mean Characteristics of Workers by Firm Size and External Financial Dependence Before the Recession

	External Financial Dependence						
	Low			High			
Firm size:	Small	Large	Diff.	Small	Large	Diff.	Diff.-Diff.
	(1)	(2)	(3)	(4)	(5)	(6)	(7)
Age (years)	41.75	39.60	2.15	41.13	39.88	1.25	-.90
			(.87)**			(.71)*	(1.12)
Proportion male	.59	.60	-.01	.70	.67	.03	.04
			(.04)			(.03)	(.05)
Proportion white	.84	.78	.07	.86	.81	.05	-.01
			(.02)***			(.02)***	(.03)
Proportion high-school dropouts	.13	.14	-.01	.15	.11	.04	.05
			(.03)			(.02)**	(.03)
Hourly wage ($2000)	14.16	16.37	-2.22	15.27	17.56	-2.29	-.07
			(.85)**			(.67)***	(1.08)
Number of observations							
Unweighted (sample)	12,131	12,007		24,164	26,480		
Weighted (population)	17.6M	17.5M		34.5M	38.3M		

Note - The table reports mean characteristics of respondents to the 2005 March Current Population Survey (CPS). The figures are reported by firm size and external financial dependence of the industry. Columns (1)-(3) include only industries with low external financial dependence, whereas columns (4)-(6) are for industries with high external financial dependence. Column (3) reports the difference between columns (1) and (2). Column (6) reports the difference between columns (4) and (5). The last column reports the difference between columns (6) and (3). Robust standard errors are in parentheses. "Small" firms have at most 99 employees. External financial dependence equals the proportion of capital expenditures financed with external funds. A negative value (low external financial dependence) indicates that firms have free cash flow. A positive value indicates that firms must issue debt or equity to finance their investment. External financial dependence is calculated at a 2-digit Standard Industrial Classification codes using mature Compustat firms for the period 1980-1996 using the procedures described in Cetorelli and Strahan (2006). All figures in the table are weighted by the sampling weights provided by the CPS. Mean values in the table are calculated based on the "unweighted" number of observations. Last row shows the sum of the sampling weights of the 2005 March CPS sample. Hourly wages are constructed by dividing annual earnings by the product of annual working weeks and usual weekly hours. We exclude wage values below the 2nd percentile and above the 98th percentile of year-specific wage distribution. Finally, we convert hourly wages to 2000 dollars using the Consumer Price Index. *, **, and *** indicate statistical significance at the 10, 5, and 1 percent levels, respectively.

Table 3 – Transition to Unemployment following the 2007 Recession:
Estimates by External Financial Dependence and Firm Size

		External Financial Dependence			
		Low		High	
	Firm size:	Small	Large	Small	Large
		(1)	(2)	(3)	(4)
		Panel A: Annual Analysis			
Recession		.025	.025	.038	.025
		(.002)***	(.002)***	(.003)***	(.002)***
Small – Large		.000		.014	
		(.003)		(.002)***	
(Small – Large)^{High} – (Small – Large)^{Low}			.013		
			(.004)***		
Observations		73,941	74,339	141,502	157,422
		Panel B: Monthly Analysis			
Recession		.027	.022	.035	.024
		(.002)***	(.002)***	(.003)***	(.002)***
Small – Large		.005		.011	
		(.003)*		(.002)***	
(Small – Large)^{High} – (Small – Large)^{Low}			.006		
			(.004)*		
Observations		160,655	171,990	371,413	405,647

Note - The dependent variable is an indicator that equals to one if a person transitioned from employment to unemployment between periods $t-1$ and t. The table reports Ordinary Least Squares estimates. Panel A is based on the annual March CPS files; panel B is based on the monthly CPS files around the March supplement. Within each panel, all estimates are from a single regression that controls for workers' characteristics and state-industry (2-digit SIC) fixed effects. Workers' characteristics include age, gender, ethnicity, and years of completed education (0-11 years, 12, 13-15, or 16). Standard errors are adjusted for clustering at state-industry (2-digit SIC) level and appear in parentheses. All estimates are weighted by probability sampling weights provided by the CPS. "Recession" equals to one in the years 2008-2010 and equals to zero in the years 2005-2007. "Small" firms have at most 99 employees. External financial dependence equals the proportion of capital expenditures financed with external funds. A negative value (low external financial dependence) indicates that firms have free cash flow. A positive value indicates that firms must issue debt or equity to finance their investment. External financial dependence is calculated at 2-digit Standard Industrial Classification codes using mature Compustat firms for the period 1980-1996 using the procedures described in Cetorelli and Strahan (2006). *, **, and *** indicate statistical significance at the 10%, 5%, and 1% levels, respectively.

Table 4 – Transition to Unemployment following the 2001 and 1990 Recessions:
Estimates by External Financial Dependence and Firm Size

		External Financial Dependence			
		Low		High	
	Firm size:	Small	Large	Small	Large
		(1)	(2)	(3)	(4)
		Panel A: 2001 Recession			
Recession		.006	.012	.006	.008
		(.002)**	(.002)***	(.002)***	(.002)***
Small – Large		−.007		−.003	
		(.002)***		(.002)	
(Small – Large)^{High} – (Small – Large)^{Low}			.004		
			(.003)		
Observations		48,934	53,076	93,496	110,102
		Panel B: 1990-1991 Recession			
Recession		.015	.019	.033	.020
		(.003)***	(.003)***	(.004)***	(.002)***
Small – Large		−.004		.013	
		(.004)		(.004)***	
(Small – Large)^{High} – (Small – Large)^{Low}			.017		
			(.006)***		
Observations		42,538	45,031	88,396	97,811

Note - The dependent variable is an indicator that equals to one if a person transitioned from employment to unemployment between years $t-1$ and t. The table reports Ordinary Least Squares estimates. Within each panel, all estimates are from a single regression that controls for workers' characteristics and state-industry (2-digit SIC) fixed effects. Workers' characteristics include age, gender, ethnicity, and years of completed education (0-11 years, 12, 13-15, or 16). Standard errors are adjusted for clustering at state-industry (2-digit SIC) level and appear in parentheses. All estimates are weighted by probability sampling weights provided by the CPS. In panel A, "Recession" equals to one in the years 2001-2002 and equals to zero in the years 1998-2000. In panel B, "Recession" equals to one in the years 1991-1992 and equals to zero in the years 1988-1990. "Small" firms have at most 99 employees. External financial dependence equals the proportion of capital expenditures financed with external funds. A negative value (low external financial dependence) indicates that firms have free cash flow. A positive value indicates that firms must issue debt or equity to finance their investment. External financial dependence is calculated at 2-digit Standard Industrial Classification codes using mature Compustat firms for the period 1980-1996 using the procedures described in Cetorelli and Strahan (2006). ** and *** indicate statistical significance at the 5% and 1% levels, respectively.

Table 5 – Transition to Unemployment following the 1990 Recession
Estimates by Region, External Financial Dependence, and Firm Size

		External Financial Dependence			
		Low		High	
	Firm size:	Small	Large	Small	Large
		(1)	(2)	(3)	(4)
		Panel A: New England			
Recession		.038	.026	.080	.029
		(.009)***	(.008)***	(.015)***	(.008)***
Small – Large		.012		.051	
		(.012)		(.013)***	
(Small – Large)^{High} – (Small – Large)^{Low}			.039		
			(.018)**		
Observations		4,005	4,744	8,071	8,533
		Panel B: Rest of the U.S.			
Recession		.013	.019	.030	.019
		(.003)***	(.003)***	(.004)***	(.002)***
Small – Large		−.005		.011	
		(.004)		(.004)***	
(Small – Large)^{High} – (Small – Large)^{Low}			.016		
			(.006)***		
Observations		38,533	40,287	80,325	89,278

Note - The dependent variable is an indicator that equals to one if a person transitioned from employment to unemployment between years $t-1$ and t. Panel A includes only the following states: Connecticut, Maine, Massachusetts, New Hampshire, Rhode Island, and Vermont. Panel B excludes these states. The table reports Ordinary Least Squares estimates. Within each panel, the estimates are from a single regression that controls for workers' characteristics and state-industry (2-digit SIC) fixed effects. Workers' characteristics include age, gender, ethnicity, and years of completed education (0-11 years, 12, 13-15, or 16). The table reports Ordinary Least Squares estimates. Standard errors are adjusted for clustering at state-industry (2-digit SIC) level and appear in parentheses. All estimates are weighted by probability sampling weights provided by the CPS. "Recession" equals to one in the years 1991-1992 and equals to zero in the years 1988-1990. "Small" firms have at most 99 employees. External financial dependence equals the proportion of capital expenditures financed with external funds. A negative value (low external financial dependence) indicates that firms have free cash flow. A positive value indicates that firms must issue debt or equity to finance their investment. External financial dependence is calculated at 2-digit Standard Industrial Classification codes using mature Compustat firms for the period 1980-1996 using the procedures described in Cetorelli and Strahan (2006). ** and *** indicate statistical significance at the 5% and 1% levels, respectively.

Table 6 – Transition to Unemployment following the 2007 Recession:
Estimates by Bank Dependence and Firm Size

		Bank Dependence			
		Low		High	
	Firm size:	Small	Large	Small	Large
		(1)	(2)	(3)	(4)
		Panel A: Annual Analysis			
Recession		.024	.019	.047	.033
		(.002)***	(.002)***	(.003)***	(.003)***
Small – Large		.004		.015	
		(.002)*		(.003)***	
(Small – Large)^{High} – (Small – Large)^{Low}			.010		
			(.004)**		
Observations		122,114	136,683	93,329	95,078
		Panel B: Monthly Analysis			
Recession		.022	.018	.046	.032
		(.002)***	(.002)***	(.003)***	(.003)***
Small – Large		.004		.014	
		(.002)**		(.003)***	
(Small – Large)^{High} – (Small – Large)^{Low}			.010		
			(.003)**		
Observations		294,434	338,677	237,634	238,960

Note - The dependent variable is an indicator that equals to one if a person transitioned from employment to unemployment between years t-1 and t. The table reports Ordinary Least Squares estimates. Panel A is based on March CPS files; panel B is based on monthly CPS files. Within each panel, all estimates are from a single regression that controls for workers' characteristics and state-industry (2-digit SIC) fixed effects. Workers' characteristics include age, gender, ethnicity, and years of completed education (0-11 years, 12, 13-15, or 16). Standard errors are adjusted for clustering at state-industry (2-digit SIC) level and appear in parentheses. All estimates are weighted by probability sampling weights provided by the CPS. "Recession" equals to one in the years 2008-2010 and equals to zero in the years 2005-2007. "Small" firms have at most 99 employees. Bank dependence is the share of assets financed with debt. We use the 1998 Survey of Small Business Finance (SSBF) to calculate measures of bank dependence for each 2-digit SIC industry. Industries with "low" bank dependence are industries with below median share of assets financed with debt. "High" bank dependence industries have above median share of assets financed with debt. *, **, and *** indicate statistical significance at the 10%, 5%, and 1% levels, respectively.

Table 7 – The Impact of the December 2007 Recession on Log Establishments Per Capita

Firm size:	External Financial Dependence			
	Low		High	
	Small	Large	Small	Large
	(1)	(2)	(3)	(4)
Recession	−.035	−.036	−.052	−.040
	(.005)***	(.004)***	(.002)***	(.003)***
Small − Large	.001		−.012	
	(.005)		(.003)***	
(Small − Large)^{High} − (Small − Large)^{Low}		−.013		
		(.006)**		
Observations	37,635	30,108	67,210	53,768

Note – The dependent variable is the natural logarithm of the number of establishment per capita in an industry/state/year. The table reports Ordinary Least Squares estimates. All estimates are from a single regression that controls for state-industry (3-digit NAICS) fixed effects. Standard errors are adjusted for clustering at the state-industry (3-digit NAICS) level and appear in parentheses. "Recession" equals to one in the years 2008-09 and equals to zero in the years 2005-07. "Small" firms have at most 99 employees. External financial dependence equals the proportion of capital expenditures financed with external funds. A negative value (low external financial dependence) indicates that firms have free cash flow. A positive value indicates that firms must issue debt or equity to finance their investment. External financial dependence is calculated at a 2-digit Standard Industrial Classification codes using mature Compustat firms for the period 1980-1996 using the procedures described in Cetorelli and Strahan (2006). The mapping between the industrial codes in Compustat and the industrial codes in the County Business Patterns is detailed in the Appendix Table 3. Number of establishments is from County Business Patterns for the years 2005-2009. Population estimates are from the U.S. Census Bureau. ** and *** indicate statistical significance at the 5% and 1% levels, respectively.

Appendix Table A.1 – Additional Robustness Tests

	External Financial Dependence			
	Low		High	
Firm Size:	Small	Large	Small	Large
	(1)	(2)	(3)	(4)
	Panel A: Dep. Variable is Transition to Non-Employment			
Recession	.024	.020	.034	.021
	(.003)***	(.003)***	(.003)***	(.002)***
Small – Large	.004		.013	
	(.004)		(.003)***	
(Small – Large)^{High} – (Small – Large)^{Low}		.009		
		(.005)*		
Observations	79,142	78,710	152,544	167,853
	Panel B: Construction Sector is Excluded			
Recession	.025	.025	.028	.020
	(.002)***	(.002)***	(.002)***	(.002)***
Small – Large	.000		.008	
	(.003)		(.002)***	
(Small – Large)^{High} – (Small – Large)^{Low}		.008		
		(.004)*		
Observations	73,941	74,339	106,058	148,212

Note –Panel A is different from the results reported in Table 3 in that the dependent variable is an indicator that equals to one if a person transitioned from employment to non-employment (unemployment or out of the labor force) between year $t-1$ and t. The table reports Ordinary Least Squares estimates. Panel B is identical to the specifications in panel A of Table 3, except the exclusion of the construction sector. All estimates are from a single regression that controls for workers' characteristics and state-industry (2-digit SIC) fixed effects. Workers' characteristics include age, gender, ethnicity, and years of completed education (0-11 years, 12, 13-15, or 16). Standard errors are adjusted for clustering at state-industry (2-digit SIC) level and appear in parentheses. All estimates are weighted by probability sampling weights provided by the CPS. "Recession" equals to one in the years 2008-2010 and equals to zero in the years 2005-2007. "Small" firms have at most 99 employees. External financial dependence equals the proportion of capital expenditures financed with external funds. A negative value (low external financial dependence) indicates that firms have free cash flow. A positive value indicates that firms must issue debt or equity to finance their investment. External financial dependence is calculated at 2-digit Standard Industrial Classification codes using mature Compustat firms for the period 1980-1996 using the procedures described in Cetorelli and Strahan (2006). * and *** indicate statistical significance at the 10% and 1% levels, respectively.

Appendix Table A.2 – External Financial Dependence by Industrial Sectors

Industry (Low External Financial Dependence)	SIC	EFD	Num. of obs. Small	Large
Forestry	08	-4.63	52	8
Insurance carriers	63	-3.96	3,032	6,898
Leather and leather products	31	-0.96	125	168
Tobacco products	21	-0.92	11	83
Apparel and other finished products made from fabrics and similar materials	23	-0.61	729	526
Educational services	82	-0.55	11,744	11,236
Security, commodity brokers, and services	62	-0.44	1,815	2,792
Social services	83	-0.43	7,277	3,696
Miscellaneous repair services	76	-0.25	2,160	491
Food and kindred products	20	-0.24	1,507	6,133
Fabricated metal products, except machinery and transportation equipment	34	-0.24	2,796	2,413
Furniture and fixtures	25	-0.23	1,243	1,281
Stone, clay, glass, and concrete products	32	-0.20	969	1,128
Miscellaneous manufacturing industries	39	-0.20	1,440	1,399
Apparel and accessory stores	56	-0.16	1,668	2,605
Business services	73	-0.16	18,622	16,536
Local and suburban transit and interurban highway passenger transportation	41	-0.12	1,104	1,246
Personal services	72	-0.12	6,911	1,120
Printing, publishing, and allied industries	27	-0.07	2,631	3,116
Communications	48	-0.07	1,351	5,552
Engineering, accounting, research, management, and related services	87	-0.05	5,797	3,733
Measuring, analyzing, and controlling instruments; photographic, medical, and optical goods	38	-0.04	957	2,179
Total for low external financial dependence			73,941	74,339

Note - This table reports measures of external financial dependence (EFD) for each industry at the 2-digit SIC category as well as the number of observations in the March Current Population Survey for the years 2005-2010. Numbers of observations are reported separately by firm size. "Small" firms have at most 99 employees. External financial dependence equals the proportion of capital expenditures financed with external funds. A negative value indicates that firms have free cash flow, whereas a positive value indicates that firms must issue debt or equity to finance their investment. External financial dependence is calculated using mature COMPUSTAT firms for the period 1980-1996. Mature firms are firms that have been on Compustat at least 10 years.

Appendix Table A.2 – External Financial Dependence by Industrial Sectors (cont.)

Industry (High External Financial Dependence)	SIC	EFD	Num. of obs. Small	Num. of obs. Large
Transportation equipment	37	0.00	1,236	7,213
Transportation services	47	0.01	1,189	1,003
Industrial and commercial machinery and computer equipment	35	0.01	1,756	4,030
Primary metal industries	33	0.03	592	1,394
Railroad transportation	40	0.04	91	966
Lumber and wood products, except furniture	24	0.04	1,490	993
Rubber and miscellaneous plastics products	30	0.04	133	498
Mining and quarrying of nonmetallic minerals, except fuels	14	0.05	885	1,602
Paper and allied products	26	0.06	315	1,363
Petroleum refining and related industries	29	0.09	95	523
Wholesale trade: non-durable goods	51	0.10	2,329	3,636
Textile mill products	22	0.10	810	1,287
Motor freight transportation and warehousing	42	0.10	5,042	4,169
General merchandise stores	53	0.12	2,018	11,622
Coal mining	12	0.13	97	572
Miscellaneous retail	59	0.16	8,533	7,688
Food stores	54	0.16	4,056	8,445
Motion pictures	78	0.17	717	681
Amusement and recreation services	79	0.21	5,389	4,735
Electronic and other electrical equipment and components, except comp. equipment	36	0.22	1,202	4,409
Electric, gas, and sanitary services	49	0.24	1,393	3,703
Eating and drinking places	58	0.25	17,491	15,204
Chemicals and allied products	28	0.28	1,277	4,641
Fishing, hunting, and trapping	09	0.31	325	34
Wholesale trade: durable goods	50	0.32	2,304	1,946
Health services	80	0.35	19,625	34,212
Real estate	65	0.38	6,991	2,743
Hotels, rooming houses, camps, and other lodging places	70	0.38	2,020	4,921
Oil and gas extraction	13	0.40	122	271
Automotive dealers and gasoline service stations	55	0.41	6,176	4,396
Automotive repair, services, and parking	75	0.43	4,973	1,303
Building materials, hardware, garden supply, and mobile home dealers	52	0.47	2,151	2,876
Transportation by air	45	0.48	245	1,934
Construction	15-16-17	0.57	35,444	9,210
Water transportation	44	0.67	75	189
Home furniture, furnishings, and equipment stores	57	0.69	2,851	2,670
Metal mining	10	0.96	22	175
Pipelines, except natural gas	46	1.00	42	165
Total for high external financial dependence			141,502	157,422

Note - This table reports measures of external financial dependence (EFD) for each industry at the 2-digit SIC category as well as the number of observations in the March Current Population Survey for the years 2005-2010. Numbers of observations are reported separately by firm size. "Small" firms have at most 99 employees. External financial dependence equals the proportion of capital expenditures financed with external funds. A negative value indicates that firms have free cash flow, whereas a positive value indicates that firms must issue debt or equity to finance their investment. External financial dependence is calculated using mature COMPUSTAT firms for the period 1980-1996. Mature firms are firms that have been on Compustat for at least 10 years.

ONLINE APPENDIX

Table O.1 – Mapping Industrial Codes between Compustat and the County Business Patterns

Industry (2-digit SIC code)	Industry (3-digit NAICS code)
Agricultural Production – Crops (1)	Crop Production (111)
Agricultural Production – Livestock (2)	Animal Production (112)
Agricultural Services (7)	Support Activities for Agriculture and Forestry (115)
Forestry (8)	Forestry and Logging (113)
Fishing, Hunting, and Trapping (9)	Fishing, Hunting and Trapping (114)
Metal Mining (10); Coal Mining (12); Nonmetallic Minerals, except Fuels (14)	Mining, except Oil and Gas (212); Support Activities for Mining (213)
Oil and Gas Extraction (13)	Oil and Gas Extraction (211)
General Building Contractors (15)	Construction of Buildings (236)
Heavy Construction Contractors (16)	Heavy and Civil Engineering Construction (237)
Special Trade Contractors (17)	Specialty Trade Contractors (238)
Food and Kindred Products (20)	Food Manufacturing (311)
Tobacco Manufactures (21)	Beverage and Tobacco Product Manufacturing (312)
Textile Mill Products (22)	Textile Mills (313); Textile Product Mills (314)
Apparel and Other Textile Products (23)	Apparel Manufacturing (315)
Lumber and Wood Products (24)	Wood Product Manufacturing (321)
Furniture and Fixtures (25)	Furniture and Related Product Manufacturing (337)
Paper and Allied Products (26)	Paper Manufacturing (322)
Printing and Publishing (27)	Printing and Related Support Activities (323); Publishing Industries, except Internet (511); Internet Publishing and Broadcasting (516)
Chemicals and allied products (28)	Chemical Manufacturing (325)

Petroleum and coal products (29)	Petroleum and Coal Products Manufacturing (324)
Rubber and Miscellaneous Plastics Products (30)	Plastics and Rubber Products Manufacturing (326)
Leather and Leather Products (31)	Leather and Allied Product Manufacturing (316)
Stone, Clay, Glass, and Concrete Products (32)	Nonmetallic Mineral Product Manufacturing (327)
Primary Metal Industries (33)	Primary Metal Manufacturing (331)
Fabricated Metal Products (34)	Fabricated Metal Product Manufacturing (332)
Industrial Machinery and Equipment (35); Electrical and Electronic Equipment (36); Instruments and Related Products (38)	Machinery Manufacturing (333); Computer and Electronic Product Manufacturing (334); Electrical Equipment, Appliance, and Component Manufacturing (335)
Transportation Equipment (37)	Transportation Equipment Manufacturing (336)
Miscellaneous Manufacturing Industries (39)	Miscellaneous Manufacturing (339)
Railroad Transportation (40)	Rail Transportation (482)
Local and Interurban Passenger Transit (41)	Transit and Ground Passenger Transportation (485)
Motor Freight Transportation and Warehousing (42)	Truck Transportation (484); Couriers and Messengers (492); Warehousing and Storage (493)
Water Transportation (44)	Water Transportation (483)
Transportation by Air (45)	Air Transportation (481)
Pipelines, except Natural Gas (46)	Pipeline Transportation (486)
Transportation Services (47)	Support Activities for Transportation (488)
Communications (48)	Broadcasting, except Internet (515); Telecommunications (517)
Electric, Gas, and Sanitary Services (49)	Utilities (221); Waste Management and Remediation Services (562)
Wholesale Trade – Durable goods (50)	Merchant Wholesalers, Durable Goods (423); Wholesale Electronic Markets and Agents and Brokers (425)
Wholesale Trade – Nondurable Goods (51)	Merchant Wholesalers, Nondurable Goods (424)

Building Materials, Hardware, Garden Supply, and Mobile Home Dealers (52)	Building Material and Garden Equipment and Supplies Dealers (444)
General Merchandise Stores (53)	General Merchandise Stores (452)
Food Stores (54)	Food and Beverage Stores (445)
Automotive Dealers and Gasoline Service Stations (55)	Motor Vehicle and Parts Dealers (441); Gasoline Stations (447)
Apparel and Accessory Stores (56)	Clothing and Clothing Accessories Stores (448)
Furniture, Home Furnishings and Equipment Stores (57)	Furniture and Home Furnishings Stores (442); Electronics and Appliance Stores (443)
Eating and Drinking Places (58)	Food Services and Drinking Places (722)
Miscellaneous Retail (59)	Health and Personal Care Stores (446); Sporting Goods, Hobby, Book, and Music Stores (451); Miscellaneous Store Retailers (453); Non-store Retailers (454)
Security, Commodity Brokers, and Services (62)	Securities, Commodity Contracts, and Other Financial Investments and Related Activities (523)
Insurance carriers (63); Insurance Agents, Brokers, and Service (64)	Insurance Carriers and Related Activities (524)
Real Estate (65)	Real Estate (531)
Holding and Other Investment Offices (67)	Lessors of Nonfinancial Intangible Assets, except Copyrighted Works (533); Management of Companies and Enterprises (551)
Hotels, Rooming Houses, Camps, and Other Lodging Places (70)	Accommodation (721)
Personal Services (72)	Personal and Laundry Services (812)
Business Services (73)	Internet Service Providers, Web Search Portals, and Data Processing Services (518); Other Information Services (519); Rental and Leasing Services (532); Administrative and Support Services (561)
Automotive Repair, Services, and Parking (75); Miscellaneous Repair Services (76)	Repair and Maintenance (811)
Motion Pictures (78)	Motion Picture and Sound Recording Industries (512)
Amusement and Recreational Services (79)	Scenic and Sightseeing Transportation (487); Performing Arts, Spectator Sports, and Related Industries (711); Amusement, Gambling, and Recreation Industries (713)

Health Services (80)	Ambulatory Health Care Services (621); Hospitals (622); Nursing and Residential Care Facilities (623)
Educational Services (82)	Educational Services (611)
Social Services (83)	Social Assistance (624)
Museums, Art Galleries, Botanical and Zoological Garden (84)	Museums, Historical Sites, and Similar Institutions (712)
Engineering and Management Services (87)	Professional, Scientific, and Technical Services (541)

Note - The table lists the mapping of 2-digit SIC industries in Compustat to industrial codes in the County Business Patterns.

ONLINE APPENDIX

Table 0.2 – Mapping Industrial Codes between Compustat and the Current Population Survey

Industry (2-digit SIC code)	Industry (3-digit Industrial Code from the CPS)
Agricultural Production—Crops (1); Agricultural Production—Livestock (2); Agricultural Services (7)	Agriculture (105)
Forestry (8)	Forestry (116)
Fishing, hunting, and trapping (9)	Fisheries (126)
Metal mining (10)	Metal mining (206)
Coal mining (12)	Coal mining (216)
Oil and gas extraction (13)	Crude petroleum and natural gas extraction (226)
Nonmetallic minerals, except fuels (14)	Nonmetallic mining and quarrying, except fuel (236)
General Building Contractors (15); Heavy Construction Contractors (16)	Construction (246)
Food and kindred products (20)	Meat products (406); Dairy products (407); Canning and preserving fruits, vegetables, and sea foods (408); Grain-mill products (409); Bakery products (416); Confectionery and related products (417); Beverage industries (418); Miscellaneous food preparations and kindred products (419); Not specified food industries (426)
Tobacco manufactures (21)	Tobacco manufactures (429)
Textile mill products (22)	Knitting mills (436); Dyeing and finishing textiles, except knit goods (437); Carpets, rugs, and other floor coverings (438); Yarn, thread, and fabric mills (439); Miscellaneous textile mill products (446); Synthetic fibers (466)
Apparel and other textile products (23)	Apparel and accessories (448); Miscellaneous fabricated textile products (449)
Lumber and wood products (24)	Logging (306); Sawmills, planing mills, and millwork (307); Miscellaneous wood products (308)
Furniture and fixtures (25)	Furniture and fixtures (309)
Paper and allied products (26)	Pulp, paper, and paperboard mills (456); Paperboard containers and boxes (457); Miscellaneous paper and pulp products (458)
Printing and publishing (27)	Printing, publishing, and allied industries (459)
Chemicals and allied products (28)	Drugs and medicines (467); Paints, varnishes, and related products (468); Miscellaneous chemicals and allied products (469)
Petroleum and coal products (29)	Petroleum refining (476); Miscellaneous petroleum and coal products (477)

Rubber and miscellaneous plastics products (30)	Rubber products (478)
Leather and leather products (31)	Leather: tanned, curried, and finished (487); Footwear, except rubber (488); Leather products, except footwear (489)
Stone, clay, glass, and concrete products (32)	Glass and glass products (316); Cement, concrete, gypsum and plaster products (317); Structural clay products (318); Pottery and related products (319); Miscellaneous nonmetallic mineral and stone products (326)
Primary metal industries (33)	Blast furnaces, steel works, and rolling mills (336); Other primary iron and steel industries (337); Primary nonferrous industries (338); Not specified metal industries (348)
Fabricated metal products (34)	Fabricated steel products (346); Fabricated nonferrous metal products (347)
Industrial machinery and equipment (35)	Agricultural machinery and tractors (356); Office and store machines and devices (357); Miscellaneous machinery (358)
Electrical and electronic equipment (36)	Electrical machinery, equipment, and supplies (367)
Transportation equipment (37)	Motor vehicles and motor vehicle equipment (376); Aircraft and parts (377); Ship and boat building and repairing (378); Railroad and miscellaneous transportation equipment (379)
Instruments and related products (38)	Professional equipment and supplies (386); Photographic equipment and supplies (387); Watches, clocks, and clockwork-operated devices (388)
Miscellaneous manufacturing industries (39)	Miscellaneous manufacturing industries (399); Not specified manufacturing industries (499)
Railroad Transportation (40)	Railroads and railway express service (506)
Local and interurban passenger transit (41)	Street railways and bus lines (516); Taxicab service (536)
Motor freight transportation and warehousing (42)	Trucking service (526); Warehousing and storage (527)
U.S. Postal Service (43)	Postal service (906)
Water transportation (44)	Water transportation (546)
Transportation by air (45)	Air transportation (556)
Pipelines, except natural gas (46)	Petroleum and gasoline pipe lines (567)
Transportation services (47)	Services incidental to transportation (568)
Communications (48)	Telephone (578); Telegraph (579); Radio broadcasting and television (856)
Electric, gas, and sanitary services (49)	Electric light and power (586); Gas and steam supply systems (587); Electric-gas utilities (588); Water supply (596); Sanitary services (597); Other and not specified utilities (598)

Wholesale trade--durable goods (50)	Motor vehicles and equipment (606); Electrical goods, hardware, and plumbing equipment (616); Machinery, equipment, and supplies (617)
Wholesale trade--nondurable goods (51)	Drugs, chemicals, and allied products (607); Dry goods apparel (608); Food and related products (609); Petroleum products (618); Farm products--raw materials (619)
Building materials, hardware, garden supply, & mobile (52)	Hardware and farm implement stores (686); Lumber and building material retailing (687)
General merchandise stores (53)	General merchandise stores (646); Five and ten cent stores (647)
Food stores (54)	Food stores, except dairy products (636); Dairy products stores and milk retailing (637)
Automotive dealers and gasoline service stations (55)	Motor vehicles and accessories retailing (667); Gasoline service stations (668)
Apparel and accessory stores (56)	Apparel and accessories stores, except shoe (656); Shoe stores (657)
Furniture, home furnishings and equipment stores (57)	Furniture and house furnishing stores (658); Household appliance and radio stores (659)
Eating and drinking places (58)	Eating and drinking places (679)
Miscellaneous retail (59)	Drug stores (669); Liquor stores (688); Retail florists (689); Jewelry stores (696); Fuel and ice retailing (697); Miscellaneous retail stores (698); Not specified retail trade (699)
Depository Institutions (60); Non-depository Credit Institutions (61)	Banking and credit agencies (716)
Security, commodity brokers, and services (62)	Security and commodity brokerage and investment companies (726)
Insurance carriers (63)	Insurance (736)
Real estate (65)	Real estate (746)
Hotels, rooming houses, camps, and other lodging plac (70)	Hotels and lodging places (836)
Personal services (72)	Laundering, cleaning, and dyeing services (846); Dressmaking shops (847); Shoe repair shops (848); Miscellaneous personal services (849)
Business services (73)	Advertising (806); Miscellaneous business services (808)
Automotive repair, services, and parking (75)	Auto repair services and garages (816)
Miscellaneous repair services (76)	Miscellaneous repair services (817)

Motion pictures (78)	Theaters and motion pictures (857)
Amusement and recreational services (79)	Bowling alleys, and billiard and pool parlors (858)
Amusement and recreational services (79)	Miscellaneous entertainment and recreation services (859)
Health services (80)	Medical and other health services, except hospitals (868); Hospitals (869)
Legal services (81)	Legal services (879)
Educational services (82)	Educational services (888)
Social services (83)	Welfare and religious services (896)
Membership organizations (86)	Nonprofit membership organizations (897)
Engineering and management services (87)	Accounting, auditing, and bookkeeping services (807); Engineering and architectural services (898)
Private households (88)	Private households (826)
Miscellaneous services (89)	Miscellaneous professional and related services (899)
Agricultural Production--Crops (1); Agricultural Production--Livestock (2); Agricultural Services (7)	Agriculture (105)
Forestry (8)	Forestry (116)
Fishing, hunting, and trapping (9)	Fisheries (126)
Metal mining (10)	Metal mining (206)
Coal mining (12)	Coal mining (216)
Oil and gas extraction (13)	Crude petroleum and natural gas extraction (226)
Nonmetallic minerals, except fuels (14)	Nonmetallic mining and quarrying, except fuel (236)
General Building Contractors (15); Heavy Construction Contractors (16)	Construction (246)
Food and kindred products (20)	Meat products (406); Dairy products (407); Canning and preserving fruits, vegetables, and seafoods (408); Grain-mill products (409); Bakery products (416); Confectionery and related products (417); Beverage industries (418); Miscellaneous food preparations and kindred products (419); Not specified food industries (426)
Tobacco manufactures (21)	Tobacco manufactures (429)
Textile mill products (22)	Knitting mills (436); Dyeing and finishing textiles, except knit goods (437); Carpets, rugs, and other floor coverings (438); Yarn, thread, and fabric mills (439); Miscellaneous textile mill products (446); Synthetic fibers (466)

Apparel and other textile products (23)	Apparel and accessories (448); Miscellaneous fabricated textile products (449)
Lumber and wood products (24)	Logging (306); Sawmills, planing mills, and millwork (307); Misc wood products (308)
Furniture and fixtures (25)	Furniture and fixtures (309)
Paper and allied products (26)	Pulp, paper, and paperboard mills (456); Paperboard containers and boxes (457); Miscellaneous paper and pulp products (458)
Printing and publishing (27)	Printing, publishing, and allied industries (459)
Chemicals and allied products (28)	Drugs and medicines (467); Paints, varnishes, and related products (468); Miscellaneous chemicals and allied products (469)
Petroleum and coal products (29)	Petroleum refining (476); Miscellaneous petroleum and coal products (477)
Rubber and miscellaneous plastics products (30)	Rubber products (478)
Leather and leather products (31)	Leather: tanned, curried, and finished (487); Footwear, except rubber (488); Leather products, except footwear (489)
Stone, clay, glass, and concrete products (32)	Glass and glass products (316); Cement, concrete, gypsum and plaster products (317); Structural clay products (318); Pottery and related products (319); Miscellaneous nonmetallic mineral and stone products (326)
Primary metal industries (33)	Blast furnaces, steel works, and rolling mills (336); Other primary iron and steel industries (337); Primary nonferrous industries (338); Not specified metal industries (348)
Fabricated metal products (34)	Fabricated steel products (346); Fabricated nonferrous metal products (347)
Industrial machinery and equipment (35)	Agricultural machinery and tractors (356); Office and store machines and devices (357); Miscellaneous machinery (358)
Electrical and electronic equipment (36)	Electrical machinery, equipment, and supplies (367)
Transportation equipment (37)	Motor vehicles and motor vehicle equipment (376); Aircraft and parts (377); Ship and boat building and repairing (378); Railroad and miscellaneous transportation equipment (379)
Instruments and related products (38)	Professional equipment and supplies (386); Photographic equipment and supplies (387); Watches, clocks, and clockwork-operated devices (388)
Miscellaneous manufacturing industries (39)	Miscellaneous manufacturing industries (399); Not specified manufacturing industries (499)
Railroad Transportation (40)	Railroads and railway express service (506)

Local and interurban passenger transit (41)	Street railways and bus lines (516); Taxicab service (536)
Motor freight transportation and warehousing (42)	Trucking service (526); Warehousing and storage (527)
U.S. Postal Service (43)	Postal service (906)
Water transportation (44)	Water transportation (546)
Transportation by air (45)	Air transportation (556)
Pipelines, except natural gas (46)	Petroleum and gasoline pipe lines (567)
Transportation services (47)	Services incidental to transportation (568)
Communications (48)	Telephone (578); Telegraph (579); Radio broadcasting and television (856)
Electric, gas, and sanitary services (49)	Electric light and power (586); Gas and steam supply systems (587); Electric-gas utilities (588); Water supply (596); Sanitary services (597); Other and not specified utilities (598)
Wholesale trade--durable goods (50)	Motor vehicles and equipment (606); Electrical goods, hardware, and plumbing equipment (616); Machinery, equipment, and supplies (617)
Wholesale trade--nondurable goods (51)	Drugs, chemicals, and allied products (607); Dry goods apparel (608); Food and related products (609); Petroleum products (618); Farm products--raw materials (619)
Building materials, hardware, garden supply, & mobile (52)	Hardware and farm implement stores (686); Lumber and building material retailing (687)
General merchandise stores (53)	General merchandise stores (646); Five and ten cent stores (647)
Food stores (54)	Food stores, except dairy products (636); Dairy products stores and milk retailing (637)
Automotive dealers and gasoline service stations (55)	Motor vehicles and accessories retailing (667); Gasoline service stations (668)
Apparel and accessory stores (56)	Apparel and accessories stores, except shoe (656); Shoe stores (657)
Furniture, home furnishings and equipment stores (57)	Furniture and house furnishing stores (658); Household appliance and radio stores (659)
Eating and drinking places (58)	Eating and drinking places (679)
Miscellaneous retail (59)	Drug stores (669); Liquor stores (688); Retail florists (689); Jewelry stores (696); Fuel and ice retailing (697); Miscellaneous retail stores (698); Not specified retail trade (699)
Depository Institutions (60); Non-depository Credit Institutions (61)	Banking and credit agencies (716)

Security, commodity brokers, and services (62)	Security and commodity brokerage and investment companies (726)
Insurance carriers (63)	Insurance (736)
Real estate (65)	Real estate (746)
Hotels, rooming houses, camps, and other lodging places (70)	Hotels and lodging places (836)
Personal services (72)	Laundering, cleaning, and dyeing services (846); Dressmaking shops (847); Shoe repair shops (848); Miscellaneous personal services (849)
Business services (73)	Advertising (806); Miscellaneous business services (808)

Note - The table lists the mapping of 2-digit SIC industries in Compustat to the 1950 Census industrial codes in IPUMS Current Population Survey files.

www.ingramcontent.com/pod-product-compliance
Lightning Source LLC
Chambersburg PA
CBHW081905170526
45167CB00007B/3156